Precious Treasure

31 Prayers Over the Children in Your Life

AMY VAUGHAN

Precious Treasure: 31 Prayers Over the Children in Your Life

Copyright 2014
Scribble Media, LLC. All Rights Reserved.

Published by:
Scribble Media LLC
2101 West Chesterfield Blvd, C100 #66
Springfield, Missouri 65807
Phone: (417) 459-4749
Fax: (417) 763-3168
Email: **contact@scribblemedia.net**

All rights reserved. Except as indicated, no part of this book may be reproduced, stored in a retrieval system, or transmitted in any form or by any means, electronic, mechanical, photocopying, microfilming, recording, or otherwise, without express written permission of the author.

ISBN: 978-0-9908952-1-3

Library of Congress Control Number: 2015900254

Dedicated to my children:

May you have abundant life and adventure. May you grow more passionate about the things you love, give grace, spread peace, and anchor yourself to Christ as you encounter the storms and joys of life.

I love you!

CONTENTS

Chapter		Page
1	Treasure By Your Design	8
2	Investigate and Study to Gain Knowledge of Him	10
3	May They Know and Trust You	12
4	You are Refuge and Strength	14
5	Stewardship	16
6	Generous, Wise and Giving	18
7	Belong. Believe. Become.	20
8	Conviction to Stand for What is Right	22
9	Learning to Obey in Order to Learn to Lead	24
10	Fruit of the Spirit	26
11	Individuality and Purpose	28
12	Compassion in Conflict	30
13	Equipped to Follow You	32
14	Continue the Good Work You Have Started	34
15	Teach Us to Learn	36
16	Thankful for Friendship	38
17	Trusting You For Contentment	40
18	Developing Initiative	42
19	Confidence in Your Grace	44
20	Patience	46
21	Guard Against Negative, Untrue Thoughts and Words	48
22	Trusting You When We Don't Understand	50
23	Learning Forgiveness	52
24	Learning to Love. Learning to Live	54
25	Living in Love and Truth	56
26	Our Strength Comes From You	58
27	Transforming Worship	60
28	Rhythm of Rest	62
29	Our Mission Field	64
30	Learning to Be Mindful and Present	66
31	Precious Treasure	68

Foreword:

If you are like me, your children are one of your greatest treasures here on earth. Because of their great value, I spend a significant amount of time in thought and prayer over them. I have written this book as a tool for parents and caregivers to use in routine prayer over those that are most precious to us – our children.

Whether you are praying in a group and using this tool as a beginning to open up group prayer time, or as an individual praying over one specific child, I invite you to start your prayer time off with these prayers. As you use this prayer book routinely, God will likely lead you to expand the prayers written here, adapt them, and individualize them to best fit your unique situation. May they be helpful to you as you pray. May they bless you and the children in your life.

Each chapter starts with a group prayer that can be used by parents together or by a group of parents opening up prayer time over their children collectively. In following along with the opening group prayer, individuals in the group can pray over a group of children collectively. This may look like parents praying over their family of multiple children, a small group of parents praying over the children in the small group, or a church group praying over the children in the church (and beyond).

The group prayer time is followed by an individual prayer that shifts focus to a specific child. The individual prayers can still be used collectively in silent prayer as a group or in small groups to pray over individual children. The individual prayers can be adapted to list multiple children by name.

Ways to use this book:

- Parents praying together or individually over one or more children in the family.

- Small groups praying together and individually over one or more children in their small group or church.

- Churches praying collectively and individually over the children in their church and community.

I

TREASURE BY YOUR DESIGN

GROUP:

Thank you, Father, for the precious miracles you have given us, our children. The children in our lives are some of the greatest gifts we will receive on earth. In Your wisdom, you have used children to shape the future of our world. You use them to influence earthly authority and turn our hearts back to You.

Open our eyes to their worth, and give us insight into how we can be used by You as a positive tool so that our actions, attitudes, and words glorify You and draw our children to You.

INDIVIDUAL:
(replace the use of "he" with "she" and "him" with "her" to pray over individual girls)

I pray _____(child's name) begins to see more of how you designed his heart with a place only You can truly fill. Show him today how great Your love is for him.

My love is but a shallow pool compared to the vastness of Your abundant love, Lord. May _____ know more of You today, Lord. May he recognize the light of Your love and be more attracted to You as he interacts with others You've placed in his path today.

Lord, You gave him as a gift on this earth to me – one I highly treasure. Today, I trust You with his development. I trust You with his character. I trust You with his future.

He is Yours, and I recognize the richness of your gift to me as his parent/ guardian. I recognize that You will use him to shape me as a person, to file off my rough edges, and bring to light my hidden character. God, give me grace to cooperate with Your plan as you shape both of us.

- John 10:10
- Deuteronomy 6:5-7
- I Samuel 2:1-10
- I Corinthians 1:26-27; Proverbs 21:1-3
- Psalms 34

2

INVESTIGATE AND STUDY TO GAIN KNOWLEDGE OF HIM

GROUP:

Lord, You are Life! You gave us physical life, you enrich our lives abundantly, You know what we need better than we do. Your Word lights our paths as we seek to teach our children about You.

God, give us wisdom today in how to present information about You in a way that our children can investigate, consider, and get to know You. May they come to see Jesus as the greatest man who has ever walked on earth and may they come to know Him as their King of Kings and the Prince of Peace. May the gospel come alive today so that they can know that Jesus came so that we could have a relationship with You forever.

INDIVIDUAL:
(replace the use of "she" with "he" and "her" with "him" to pray over individual boys)

I pray that _____ will seek You with all her heart today. I pray she will come to crave knowledge about You that will shape her heart and her life today, Lord. May she know deeply of Your love. May she choose to investigate and study Your Word. May she hold close to her heart the knowledge that You give her.

I pray that _____ claims you as her Rock, her Sword, her Shield as she faces the adventures of today. I pray that her fear is replaced with confidence and hope in You, Lord. May she draw near to You when she is in trouble, and may she celebrate what You are teaching her today.

- Psalms 139: 13-14
- Psalms 14:2; Psalms 18:1-2; Psalms 27:1; Psalms 33:20-22; Psalms 27:5
- John 3:16; John 14:6
- Matthew 6:33

3

MAY THEY KNOW AND TRUST YOU

GROUP:

Father, in this life, there are many paths. There are many distractions. May our children be drawn to You so strongly that they seek after You with all their hearts, all their minds, and all their strength. May they value relationship with You above all else, and may they treat others with honor and respect and grow in healthy relationships with them as an overflow of their healthy relationship with You.

May you bless our children with the determination to anchor themselves to You amidst the storms and joys in this life. May they KNOW You are God. May they serve You and seek to glorify Your name. May they cling to you and learn to talk with You as their Best Friend. May they know they can count on You when it feels as if the world is against them. May they know that Your love is vast enough to absorb even the most tragic and heartbreaking moments they experience. May they know that You love them enough to discipline them and guide them toward a more abundant life and understanding. May they grow to know that You have something richer than happiness in store for them. May they have a foreshadowing of that JOY today. May they experience Your goodness and come to recognize it even in the midst of a no-good-very-bad day, Lord. May they KNOW that You are GOOD.

INDIVIDUAL:
(replace the use of "he" with "she" and "him" with "her" to pray over individual girls)

Father, may _____ know You as God today. May he trust You to shape his future today. May he trust You with his life and his decisions today.

May he treat others with compassion and with tender heartedness, just as You treat us. May he choose kindness in his interaction. May he be wise and choose to follow You even when the distractions and choices to go a different way are great. May he see the Light of Your path and follow it today, Lord.

- Ephesians 4:32
- Romans 12:9-10; Luke 2:52
- John 1:14; Colossians 1:15; Colossians 2:9
- Hebrews 12:1

4

YOU ARE REFUGE AND STRENGTH

GROUP:

We are so grateful, Lord, for the hearts of our children. We pray You protect their innocence and work through the experiences they have today to draw them closer to You. We pray that they seek to develop sharp minds and knowledge in order to grow in wisdom. We pray that they seek to develop soft hearts that they might live a life of abundant love. Give them a desire to be the hands and feet of Jesus in our community and world. Give them eyes to see one small act of service they might provide to bless another person today, Lord.

INDIVIDUAL:
(replace the use of "she" with "he" and "her" with "him" to pray over individual boys)

I am grateful for _____ today. I love her heart and the Light that I see developing in her. I pray she recognizes that she can do all that You call her to do when she looks to You for the strength to do it. May she grow in her ability to look to You as her source of strength, calm, peace, and wisdom today. May she recognize and celebrate what you are doing in her life and through her today.
May _____ turn to You as her refuge and strength, especially when she is in trouble. May she be resourceful and use what You have given her to face the storms and joys of today. May she trust You and rest in the knowledge that You have equipped her to face today. May she bring joy to those around her as they see Your light in her life today.

- Ecclesiastes 9:10
- Philippians 4:13
- Psalms 23:1
- Matthew 11:28-30

5

STEWARDSHIP

GROUP:

Lord, may we recognize the call in our lives to guide our children toward You. May we speak words of love and wisdom into their lives. May we live in a way that guides them to You.

Thank You for redeeming us, for purifying us, for reminding us of the grace in which You have poured richly over our own lives. May we reflect what You have done for us in the way in which we deal with our children today. May our eyes see what our children need from us today. May we be available and purposefully present in their lives today.

INDIVIDUAL:
(replace the use of "he" with "she" and "him" with "her" to pray over individual girls)

God, _____ is made in Your image. May he grow today in his ability to recognize the gifts and talents that You have given to him. May he strive to cooperate with Your work in him as You develop his character and his heart today. May he come to recognize the signposts You place in his life to guide his way. May he value the wisdom You bring his way through those he meets today. May he be generous in giving to others – both in sharing his possessions and in sharing himself in friendship. May he see that You love him no matter what he looks like, whether his style is "in" or "out." May he learn to be faithful as he comes to understand Your faithfulness to him.

Give _____ a heart that is fair and kind. Teach him that how he uses what You give him is more important than how many possessions he has. Show him that his greatest gift is Jesus and that all other things pale in comparison with that free gift and forever relationship. Shed light on his journey and transform his life into one that glorifies You more today than yesterday. Give him a heart to follow hard after You more today than yesterday.

- Philippians 1:3
- 1 Timothy 6:18
- Psalms 103:8
- Micah 6:8
- Acts 10:34-35

6

GENEROUS, WISE & GIVING

GROUP:

May our children be generous with all that You have provided. May they seek You as the ultimate source for what they need. May they come to understand that how they give is more important than how much they give. May they recognize that how they use what you provide is more important than the number of their earthly possessions or wealth. May they recognize that true wealth comes from you and surpasses coins, paper, and material things. May the possessions that they have never get in the way of their ability to see You first and to serve You first. May You guard their hearts against the love of money and "stuff."

INDIVIDUAL:
(replace the use of "she" with "he" and "her" with "him" to pray over individual boys)

God, give _____ wisdom in how she handles her money, her possessions, and the things she desires. May she recognize You as the provider of all that she needs. May she look to honor You with what she has – both her gifts and talents as well as her possessions.

God, I pray you give _____ a generous heart. Give her a desire to help others. Give her eyes to see where she can be Your Light in the world, where she can share Your love, and where she can be a ray of hope as others see You working in her life. Protect her today and give her a determination to follow after You today. I trust that You have her in this place, at this time, for a purpose.

Thank You for holding her close, even if she is in this place through poor decisions, apathy, or wrong choices. May You work through each and every circumstance in her life today, Lord, both those that began before today and those that are beginning based on her choices today, to mold her. Help her to develop a generous heart that is ready and willing to share.

- Proverbs 31
- Mark 12:44
- Luke 12:15
- Luke 18:22
- 1 Timothy 6:18

7

BELONG. BELIEVE. BECOME.

GROUP:
Thank you, Lord, for your mercy and kindness toward our children. We stand amazed at your great love and steadfast patience. You claim us as Yours before our behavior ever stands as representative of You. You lead us into belief despite our unbelief. You shape us into becoming even as we resist being molded into something beautiful. May You continue to work richly in our lives and the lives of our children. May Your will be done in our families and in our community. May You give our children the courage to be authentic and honest in relationships today.

INDIVIDUAL:
(replace the use of "he" with "she" and "him" with "her" to pray over individual girls)

I thank You for _____'s heart. I pray that he will know that he belongs to You and that You created him for good works, authentic relationship, and to glorify You with his gifts and talents. I pray that he learns to delight in who You have created him to be just as You delight in him as Your creation. Grow his belief in You, his relationship with You, and his knowledge of Your work in his life today. May he desire to become the man after Your heart that You have designed him to be.

- Psalms 103:8
- Acts 13:22; 1 Samuel 13:13-14
- Romans 8:28
- Acts 27:22

8

CONVICTION TO STAND FOR WHAT IS RIGHT

GROUP:

Father, I praise You for the example of Jesus who followed Your leading even when it was hard. In this world, our children may feel like they are standing alone in doing what is right. I thank you for the examples of Jesus, Daniel, Stephen, and Elijah, all of whom had the courage to do what was right in the face of extreme circumstances. May our children anchor themselves to You in the midst of life so securely that when the storms of life come, their faith in You is secure. May You stand as the Mighty Fortress in their lives that is consistent and safe no matter what life brings their way today. May the peace of Christ follow our children today wherever You might send them. May they return from their day rejoicing in You and the work You are doing in their lives.

INDIVIDUAL:
(replace the use of "she" with "he" and "her" with "him" to pray over individual boys)

May the peace of all peace be _____'s today. May she confidently follow after You. May she hear Your voice and discern Your will in the midst of today's noise. May she stand for what is right even if there are others who do not. May she never tire of doing what is right.

Thank you that You are able to bring about good and blessing in her life – even from circumstances that others did not intend for her benefit. Teach her how to worship you with her actions, her attitudes and her words today.

Give her wisdom to face each tough decision and an inner peace that confirms the Light to direct her steps. Thank you that she may make choices, but You are directing her path. I am so thankful that I can trust her life into Your hands to shift or to plant and that she is safe because she is in the center of Your will.

I rest in the knowledge that Your love won't allow her to miss Your best when she is seeking You. May she seek You today with all her heart.

- Luke 22:42; Acts 7:54; 1 Kings 18:22
- 2 Thessalonians 3:13
- John 15:5
- Psalms 37:4-6
- Isaiah 43:7; Isaiah 43:19
- Isaiah 55:8

9

LEARNING TO OBEY
IN ORDER TO LEARN TO LEAD

GROUP:

May our children recognize Your love for them today as they trust those You have put in leadership positions in their lives. May those who lead our children be aware of how precious our children are to You and realize that they answer to You for their attitudes and actions toward our children. May our children see those around them as important to You and valuable to You. May they treat those around them carefully and respectfully today. May our children delight today that You have chosen them to know of You. May they rest in the knowledge that You have gone ahead of them and will walk beside them through this day.

INDIVIDUAL:
(replace the use of "he" with "she" and "him" with "her" to pray over individual girls)

Today I pray that You will guide _____ in wisdom as he seeks to follow the leadership of those You have placed in his life. May he have rich discernment as he trusts and obeys so that he does not obey blindly, but with full confidence that

You have his best interests at heart. May he treat others with fairness and celebrate those who are different than he is. May he show others the love that You continually show him. May his heart be soft to Your direction and may he recognize Truth when he encounters it. May he quickly identify circumstances that are unhealthy and distractions that are not in his best interest and have the ability to shift his attention back to healthy things.

- Hebrews 13:17
- James 2:7
- Luke 10:33
- Acts 10:34-35

10

FRUIT OF THE SPIRIT

GROUP:

Today, we invite the Holy Spirit to produce fruit in the lives of our children – love, joy, peace, patience, kindness, goodness, faithfulness, gentleness, and self-control. May our children learn to desire more of these things on a daily basis. May they begin to recognize these qualities in others and value them. May they realize that the more they love God, the more they have the capacity to love others. May their lives be so full of grace and fruit that there is no room for pride, conceit, jealousy, or malice. May they find relationships that provide positive energy and fruit so that they might reflect that positivity and fruit to others that they meet. May they be trustworthy in friendship and love their friends loyally and deeply.

INDIVIDUAL:
(replace the use of "she" with "he" and "her" with "him" to pray over individual boys)

I pray a life full of fruit for _____. May she experience a depth of love that inspires her to love abundantly. May she experience joy unspeakable and everlasting. May she know the peace of all peace that passes all understanding. May she have patience even in extreme situations. May she value and develop kindness toward herself and others. May she cling to what is good and be faithful in all that is set before her to do. May she be faithful and gentle toward others in her life. May she learn self-control so that she can choose to respond with kindness and love consistently. May all of these qualities grow in her as a result of Your good work in her life and heart. May she be quick to show forgiveness and grace.

- Matthew 22:37-40
- Galatians 5:22-26
- John 15:12

11

INDIVIDUALITY AND PURPOSE

GROUP:

Father God, we thank you for the fact that You give us the opportunity to join You in the good that You are doing in this world. Thank you for responsibility and experiences that we initially think are for other people that You are actually using equally to change and shape us. May our children choose to join You in Your work today. May they see that You give wisdom, and may they turn to you as a first resource instead of a last resort. May they discover more about who You created them to be today so that they may be a light to those around them today as they embrace their unique gifts and talents and personality. May they praise You because of the wonderful way You created them.

INDIVIDUAL:
(replace the use of "he" with "she" and "him" with "her" to pray over individual girls)

Lord, work in _____ today. Grow his understanding of the way You designed him. May he embrace his personality and his gifts and talents and deploy them today in Your service. May he find purpose and joy in Your creation.

Teach _____ to look for what You are doing and join You there. Teach him to link arms with others and work with them in order to accomplish more together. Teach him to value the input that others bring to a group project or team effort. Build trustworthiness in him as he looks to trust You. May he see the race set before him today and give his all today. May he bless others as he works alongside them today. May he learn more of You today and how to glorify You with his actions, attitudes, and words.

- Ecclesiastes 4:9
- Luke 16:10
- Daniel 6:4
- Exodus 35:35
- Nehemiah 2:18
- Mathew 7:12
- 1 John 4:16
- Psalms 139:14

12

COMPASSIONATE IN CONFLICT

GROUP:

Teach our children to be compassionate and skilled at communicating to resolve conflict, Lord. Teach them to be kind in their words and actions today. Don't let them remain in conflict with another if resolution and reconciliation is possible today. Show them the value in forgiving others and reconciling differences. Show them where You are at work even in the pain and conflict that is in their lives.

Show them how to put on a cloak of compassion toward others. Teach them to be fair in their interaction with others today, especially those they lead. Work through their relationships today to do great and wonderful things!

INDIVIDUAL:
(replace the use of "she" with "he" and "her" with "him" to pray over individual boys)

God, be with _____ today as she navigates the world of relationships and conflict. Be with her as she seeks to honor You in how she treats others today.

Give her a heart of forgiveness and a desire to reconcile her differences with others. Show her where You are working for her good through the pain and conflict she experiences.

Give her compassion toward others and a heart that seeks to be fair in her dealings with others today. Bless her relationships and interaction with others. May her relationships be healthy. May her dealings with others be fair and honest. May her heart for others be compassionate and giving. May she seek to honor You in the way You designed her today.

- Ephesians 4:32
- 2 Corinthians 1:4
- Colossians 3:12
- Ephesians 4:26-27

13

EQUIPPED TO FOLLOW YOU

GROUP:

Lord, we are so grateful that You have equipped our children to face what is set before them today. You have equipped them with skills and talents that are different than our own. Help us see them in the light of who You have created them to be today and not only in the light of who we are.

Help us to recognize and trust Your work in their lives today. Help us to join You in gently correcting and disciplining our children in love today. Help us to teach them to run the race of life with all their hearts as You teach us to do the same.

Help us to take care of them and teach them to take care of themselves because we belong to You – help us to honor You in the way we treat ourselves and others. Help us as a family and community of believers to see what's right and keep doing it.

INDIVIDUAL:
(replace the use of "he" with "she" and "him" with "her" to pray over individual girls)

Thank you, God, for the way you have equipped _____ to face this day and the activities that You will bring his way today.

Thank you that You will show him how to find You when he seeks You. Soften him so he can be teachable today as he learns to do what needs to be done even when he doesn't feel like doing it.

Remind him to honor himself and others because we belong to You. Teach him to take care in how he treats his own body and the way that he treats others today.

Thank you for the good work You are doing in his life. Help that work spill over into his relationships so that he makes a practice of treating others better than expected. May he have a heart to go the extra mile in his work and in his relationships. May his heart grow in strength and compassion and wisdom as he interacts with others today. May he look to You when he is unsure of how to respond. May he see value in healthy living as he exercises and eats today.

- Matthew 7:12
- Colossians 3:23
- Genesis 24:14
- John 13:15
- Psalms 119:32
- 1 Corinthians 6:18
- Daniel 1:8

14

CONTINUE THE GOOD WORK YOU HAVE STARTED

GROUP:

Thank you, God, that You work in our children's lives even when they are sidetracked and distracted. Thank you that You can work through all circumstances for their good, even through disappointing choices that they make or the natural consequences of unwise decisions.

We are so thankful that You are at work in all of the joy and the sorrows our children face. We are thankful that the battle for their minds and hearts is ultimately Yours – that they are ultimately Yours and that You only ask us to cooperate with what You are doing.

We are so relieved that You are not dependent on us to shape our child's future and success, but that You allow us the opportunity to shepherd Your precious treasure and serve as the stewards of Your treasure. We are thankful that You continue the good work You have begun in our children, just as You do in our own lives. Give us wisdom as we are Your vessels in our children's lives to say or not say, to do or not do, to honor You in how we deal with them today.

INDIVIDUAL:
(replace the use of "she" with "he" and "her" with "him" to pray over individual boys)

God, You have good plans for _____. Help me to recognize Your work in her life today and to cooperate with what You are doing.

Give me wisdom in what to say or not say to her as she navigates the circumstances in her day today. Give me wisdom in how to come alongside her and guide her. Protect her today from my own bias and experience. Protect her from any judgmental or wrong attitudes and actions I might have that would negatively influence her today.

Give me wisdom in how to walk beside her today as her leader, living authentically and honestly, yet full of grace and love, so she might be drawn to You.

- James 1:2-4
- Romans 8:28-29
- Proverbs 14:2
- 2 Chronicles 20:15
- Ecclesiastes 3:7

15

TEACH US TO LEARN

GROUP:

Thank you, God, for the gift of learning for our children. Thank you that whether they are learning a new routine or learning knowledge, You are blessing them today. Thank you that if they encounter a situation they don't understand or need to act but don't know what to do, all they have to do is approach You and You will give them wisdom for today.

Help them understand that their wisdom and knowledge is a gift directly from You. Help them to love You above all else – even above their own wisdom and understanding. Help them to recognize You as the giver of all good things today. Help them to learn what they need to know to face today's circumstances and relationships. Help them to look beyond the knowledge and possessions You have given them in order to see others today. Help them to be generous in giving of themselves today.

INDIVIDUAL:
(replace the use of "he" with "she" and "him" with "her" to pray over individual girls)

Thank you, Lord, for _____'s mind. Thank you that you have equipped him to learn what he needs to learn in order to serve You and to enjoy the life You have given to him today.

Give him eyes to see beyond himself today, yet wisdom to take care of both himself and others. Give him the wisdom of Solomon and help him to enjoy his work today and the friends You bring into his path.

Help him to appreciate those that are wired differently than he is and to listen to wise counsel when and where he finds it. Teach him a deep respect for You and for Your creation. Help him to delight in doing good and give him endurance as he strives to keep pressing forward in this life. Give him inspiration and motivation today. Give him direction and purpose.

- Proverbs 1:7
- 1 Kings 3:11
- Matthew 13:9
- Galatians 6:9

16

THANKFUL FOR FRIENDSHIP

GROUP:

Thank you, God, for friendship. Thank you that we don't walk alone in this life. Thank you that You plan for our children to have friends and deep interpersonal connection with others.

Give our children patience and understanding when dealing with friends. Give them a heart for relationship and the endurance to stick with the lifelong friendships that You provide.

Plant seeds of righteousness and truth in our children and their friends today. Give them new starts where they need them. Give them warm smiles and soft hearts, protected by wisdom and discernment and knowledge of You.

Arrange their day so that they are available to help others who need them today. Bless them as they go about their day and interact with friends.

Thank you, God, that You give no weight to status or position, but that You see the heart and are not distracted by worldly possessions. May our children do the same as they approach friendships. May they value the heart of their friends and not be distracted by status, position or possessions in their friendships.

INDIVIDUAL:
(replace the use of "she" with "he" and "her" with "him" to pray over individual boys)

Today, Lord, I pray that you will bring special connection with a friend to _____ today. I pray that she will build beautiful memories with someone she trusts and enjoys today. I pray that You will give her wisdom in choosing who she spends time with and who she connects with deeply.

I pray that You will protect her from those that would lead her astray. Please give her healthy friendships. May she see her friends clearly and choose them wisely. May she stick by them loyally and love them fiercely.

- Proverbs 17:17
- Proverbs 13:20
- 1 Samuel 18:1-4
- Galatians 6:7-10

17

TRUSTING YOU FOR CONTENTMENT

GROUP:

We are so relieved that we can rest in Your excellent creation. We are so thankful that You took the same care and precision in creating our children that You did in creating the Universe.

Thank you that we can trust You in Your wisdom as You grow, lead, develop, and direct our children. Thank you for what you have given us in our children. May we delight in them and appreciate the diversity of Your creation in our family and community.

May we spend time building relationships and memories with our children that will last a lifetime today and each day from now on. May we value the gift of our children even during the mundane of every day. May we be content in who You made them to be and cease striving to make them into something we think might be better.

Forgive us when we attempt to improve upon Your excellent design instead of supporting Your plan for our children. Teach us to respect Your precious treasure with the words and actions we use in interaction with them today.

INDIVIDUAL:
(replace the use of "he" with "she" and "him" with "her" to pray over individual girls)

God, give _____ contentment today. Help him rest and bloom in the place where You have planted him today. Help him embrace who You have made him and grow to be all he can be.

Help him to stand in awe of You and how You designed him. Help him to embrace his uniqueness and find the work and the relationships that feed his soul. Help him to learn to do more than simply exist and endure. Help him to find joy and fulfillment in his day. Help him to rest in You and learn to listen to Your voice and KNOW you. Help him to be content in any circumstance because his happiness is not based in the circumstance but in the security of his relationship with You. May You draw him ever closer to Yourself today and each day from now on.

- Matthew 6:19
- Romans 13:1
- 1 Peter 2:17

Philippians 4:11-12
1 Samuel 24:17
Ecclesiastes 5:18-20

18

DEVELOPING INITIATIVE

GROUP:

God, we are so thankful that You delight in both the introverted and the extroverted, in both the quiet leader and the bold one who proclaims Your truth.

We ask You to give our children initiative, whether it is to be used "behind the scenes" in a quiet way or to boldly lead out front of a group. We ask that You inspire our children to jump into life wholeheartedly and enjoy it. We ask that they would enjoy the "doing" in life and find purpose in the work You set before them.

We ask that they would embrace the rest and relaxation You bring, but not dwell there forever. We ask that You would help them find their rhythm of work, play, rest, relationship, and serving, and find balance and health today in those things. Guard their hearts and minds today with Your peace that is beyond our understanding.

INDIVIDUAL:
(replace the use of "she" with "he" and "her" with "him" to pray over individual boys)

May _____ develop initiative today as she navigates her day. Give her courage to do what she knows is right. Give her wisdom and understanding to time her actions well so that she might experience greater success.

Teach her the rhythm of life You have for her and help her balance work, play, rest, relationships and service today. Meet her right where she is in her learning and in her doing and continue Your work in her life today. Inspire her today to have new ideas and plans and give her the initiative to begin and follow those dreams You have given. May she recognize You as the giver of all of the good things in her life and cling to You through the storms and adventures of the day.

- Philippians 4:7
- I Corinthians 12:4
- Philippians 2:4
- Judges 6:15
- I Samuel 16:7
- I Corinthians 12:1-11
- Matthew 3:3

19

CONFIDENCE IN YOUR GRACE

GROUP:

God, we pray that our children feel called to follow You and glorify You today. We pray that they are sensitive to Your leading in their lives today. We pray that they grow in their desire to praise You to the point that it becomes second nature and a rhythm that they embrace.

We pray that they seek positive influences in their lives today. We pray that they value the good gifts You have given. We pray that they find joy in all of life's circumstances, especially those that are not in their control to change.

Give them a confidence in Your grace and love that surpasses their human knowledge and understanding. Give them faith to believe that You have a reason for the circumstances they are in even if they do not see the reason or understand.

Give them a desire to follow you, not in perfectionism, but in authenticity. Help them to see the mistakes they make today as opportunities to choose a different way. Help them to embrace the adventure You have set before them with anticipation and excitement, knowing that You have good things in store for them during this journey.

INDIVIDUAL:
(replace the use of "he" with "she" and "him" with "her" to pray over individual girls)

I pray that _____ feels Your hand in his life today. May he see how You are actively working to direct his path today. Help him grow in his desire to communicate with You and follow Your lead to the point that it becomes a natural rhythm for him to look to You.

Lord, make that rhythm as natural and unconscious as breathing for him today. Help him to learn from his mistakes and honor You in how he redirects following a misstep. Help him to see Your guidance and discipline as present in his life because of Your great love for him. Help him be responsive and teachable today.

- Psalms 100:1-2
- Ephesians 5:15-16
- Genesis 1:29
- Ephesians 5:16
- Romans 8:38
- Matthew 6:33

20

PATIENCE

GROUP:

We are thankful for the excitement and energy of youth. We are thankful that they are naturally driven to find answers and to seek Truth.

We welcome the challenge to think through why we believe what we believe so that we might answer their questions and correct our own walk if we have drifted due to inattention or complacency. We realize that what You are doing in our children's lives is not about us. In some circumstances You have a plan where their fruit or work may surpass our own.
We welcome Your plan for the lives of ourselves and our children. We embrace the plans You have for them and for us. May we be patient as we wait to see what Your plan entails. Give our children patience as they wish to know all the answers to the questions they have today.

May they trust You to show them answers over time, knowing that You know what their hearts and minds can digest today and that You are actively preparing them to know and understand the answers to the questions they ask today.

INDIVIDUAL:
(replace the use of "she" with "he" and "her" with "him" to pray over individual boys)

God, give _____ patience today as she encounters questions and seeks answers. May she learn to wait to fully know and understand what she wants to know now. May she trust that You are preparing her to learn character and not just get quick answers to her questions.

Help her understand that gaining wisdom takes time. May she see your love for her today. May she not worry about tomorrow, but embrace the joy in living today. May she be anxious in nothing, but turn to You in every circumstance, trusting Your love for her and Your provision. May she give You her whole heart and trust and consult You before sharing her heart with others. Prepare her heart for both today and her future.

- Proverbs 25:28
- Matthew 7:25-34
- Philippians 4:19
- Philippians 4:6-7

21

GUARD AGAINST NEGATIVE, UNTRUE THOUGHTS & WORDS

GROUP:

Today we put our trust and confidence in You, God, as You guard and protect our children. We honor Your plan for their lives and ours. We ask You to guard against negative, untrue thoughts and words in their lives and ours as we seek You today.

May we all find our identity in You and guard against leading others astray by giving too much weight to our knowledge or falling into a pattern of self-righteousness. May we put on the belt of Truth today and body armor of Your righteousness today.

May we recognize that you desire for us to shed our dirty clothes and dark deeds and put on the shining armor of right living, not because You are holding us back or restricting our fun in this life, but because You desire for us to live life to the fullest and You are protecting us from the emptiness of those shallow moments. May we delight in honoring others today and acting toward them in loving kindness.

INDIVIDUAL:
(replace the use of "he" with "she" and "him" with "her" to pray over individual girls)

May _____ find his confidence in You today, Lord. May he acknowledge You and Your work in his life and circumstances today. May You guard him against negative, untrue thoughts and words today.

May he seek Your truth and find his self-worth in positive ways without elevating himself above others. May he delight in his knowledge of You but never use his knowledge as a weapon or as a crutch in relationships with others. May he discover knew depths to Your love for him and his love for others today. May he genuinely connect with You and with others today.

- Proverbs 3:5-6
- Romans 12:9-13
- Romans 13:11-14
- Ephesians 6

22

TRUSTING YOU WHEN WE DON'T UNDERSTAND

GROUP:

Father, give us confidence in You as we face this day with our children. We pray You will guard against apathy, complacency, worry, anxiety, and the fear of the mystery in life that we do not understand.

Give us shoes of peace and help us be prepared for today by putting our shoes on. Give us a shield of faith and a helmet of salvation with a sword powered by Your Holy Spirit today. Help our children to be protected by the armor You provide for them and help them to cooperate with Your protection today. Give them faith and peace that surpasses what they understand and give them wisdom to turn toward You when life gets bumpy. Give our children a confidence that You are at work in their lives today. Give us a confidence that You are at work in their lives and circumstances today. We believe You will use the circumstances in their lives for their good and to draw them to You.

INDIVIDUAL:
(replace the use of "she" with "he" and "her" with "him" to pray over individual boys)

Guard _____'s heart in times where she is vulnerable to fear of the unknown, anxiety, worry, apathy, or complacency. Give her a healthy perspective on the world around her and give her a heart of compassion and kindness toward those that she meets today.

Give her faith as she will encounter situations that are beyond her understanding. When she encounters hard things today, prompt her to go back to what she knows about You as her rock solid foundation. Give her the tools today to continue building her life around Your truth and help her to set her life in a rock solid relationship with You that cannot be swept away by any of the events she encounters today. May her adventure be challenging, exciting and fun and may she cling to You as she weathers the storms in life that are inevitable.

- Ephesians 6
- Romans 12:10
- Romans 8:28
- Proverbs 3:5-6
- Acts 27:25
- Genesis 9:13
- 1 Corinthians 11:24

23

LEARNING FORGIVENESS

GROUP:

God, we confess that we have made mistakes in guiding our children and those mistakes may have affected their progress toward You at times. We recognize that our actions and words have not always been what we wish they were in hindsight.

We ask that You cover our mistakes with Your grace in the lives of our children. Protect them from the things that hinder them in their relationship with You. May we be bold in asking for forgiveness when needed and may we be careful not to judge others when we have been wrong so often, too.

May we give out grace as freely as You do. May we welcome our children with open arms no matter what. May we be the first to apologize and the first to forgive wrongs toward us. May we tap into the depth and breadth of Your love today for our children. May we grow as a people and as a community because of our experience with the children in our lives. Thank you for using them to shape us to look more like Jesus.

INDIVIDUAL:

(replace the use of "he" with "she" and "him" with "her" to pray over individual girls)

May _____ seek after You despite those who have failed him here on earth. May he strive to embrace goodness despite the times he has not been treated well by others. May he be quick to forgive and slow to judge. May he have security in the relationships at home that surpass any he can find in the rest of the world. May he have faith to follow You today and grow in his confidence that You have him and his life circumstances in the palm of Your hand. May he listen as You lead today and may he be responsive.

- 2 Thessalonians 3:13
- Colossians 3:13
- John 8:7
- Matthew 5:24
- Matthew 22:37-39
- Hebrews 11:1

24

LEARNING TO LOVE, LEARNING TO LIVE

GROUP:

May we be champions of our children today as we engage with them in everyday tasks. May we celebrate their strengths and support their weaknesses so that they might know we believe in them and believe in their ability to succeed in this life.

May they feel loved for who they are and celebrated for how You designed them to be. May our love be a direct reflection of Your love today – may it be rich and full and deep.

Thank you that the goodness that You give to us comes freely and does not have to be earned. Thank you that You died, not to make us GOOD, but to bring us ALIVE.

INDIVIDUAL:
(replace the use of "she" with "he" and "her" with "him" to pray over individual boys)

_____ is a beautiful example of Your creation, Lord. May I recognize her individual gifts, talents and growing character today. May I celebrate the work You are doing in her and through her to influence others for good.

May she realize that her purpose on this earth is not be GOOD, but to be ALIVE and glorify You. You are easy to please and slow to anger. May my time and affection be readily available to _____ today. May she feel loved and cherished as my most precious treasure on earth today. May she see my correction or guidance in light of my love for her and realize that it is out of love that I desire to see her learn so she can have a full abundant life.

- Matthew 22:37-40
- Galatians 2:16
- Galatians 2:21
- John 15:12

25

LIVING IN LOVE AND TRUTH

GROUP:

In a world where truth and love and integrity and honesty are thrown around like candy, yet rarely genuinely practiced, we pray that You will protect our children from embracing shallow replicas of what these words really mean.

We pray that You will give them (and us) experience with genuine truth, love, integrity, and honesty so that we recognize their presence and can discern the sincerity of words and acts as we encounter them. May we each learn to wisely spend our time.

May we use technology as a tool to enhance our ability to complete work and build relationships and not as a substitute for living life to the fullest. Guard the hearts and minds of our children from the unhealthy things that are available through technology, in music, on the television, and in movies.

May they be wise in what they watch. May our children be active and not passive today as they approach their day. May they seek to go out and discover new things about life and about themselves instead of waiting for life to find them.

INDIVIDUAL:
(replace the use of "he" with "she" and "him" with "her" to pray over individual girls)

May _____ know how valuable he is today. May he realize that he is too valuable to be unhealthy or unsafe in his actions today. May he realize that the choices he makes in what he watches and listens to on-line and through technology affect his day.

May he choose to engage in activities that build his skills and enhance his positive attitudes, actions and words. May he actively pursue excellence and health today. May he love others even when he has to set aside what is convenient to do so. Help him value Your perspective over his own today and help me to support him in his growing independence.

- Matthew 22:37-39
- 2 John
- John 21:17

26

OUR STRENGTH COMES FROM YOU

GROUP:

Father God, we ask You to give our children physical, emotional, and spiritual strength today. Help them to exercise self-control and give them reservoirs of strength to draw from as they face the circumstances of their day today.

May You continue to give them challenges that build their faith and trust in You. May they quickly recognize that secondary things can never satisfy core longings – only You can satisfy what our souls need most.

We ask that You reveal Yourself to our children and draw them into relationship with You. May they develop a relationship with You that is the bedrock of their lives. The resulting joy will be something that cannot be taken from them or shaken by life's happenings. We pray this for our children in Your name.

INDIVIDUAL:
(replace the use of "she" with "he" and "her" with "him" to pray over individual boys)

May _____ celebrate her relationship with You today, Lord. May she recognize the awesomeness of Your creation and realize that she has the opportunity to delight in Your plan and be a part of the beauty around her.

Give her eyes to recognize Your work and an awareness of the beauty that surrounds her today. May she realize the shallow substitutes that she has used to satisfy her core longings and help her choose to refocus on You.

Only You can truly satisfy her soul and in You she will find the answers that she seeks. Give her strength physically, emotionally, and spiritually today so that she might develop and train for the life that lays ahead of her. Teach her to pause and recognize where You are acting in her life regularly so that she might be ready to cooperate when she hears You speak directly into her life.

- Zephaniah 3:17
- Psalms 16:7,9,11
- Psalms 139:14
- Lamentations 3:20-24

27

TRANSFORMING WORSHIP

GROUP:

God, we pray today that our children experience life transforming worship. We pray that they come to know the power by which they are saved, the strength that holds them secure in their salvation. We pray they find their worth and meaning based in You. We pray that our children "wake up" fully and choose to be present during the events of the day. We pray that they are mindful of Your work in their lives and in the lives of others around them today.

We pray that our children learn to discern Your voice and activity in them and the world around them today and that they take notice so that they may join You in what You are doing.

INDIVIDUAL:
(replace the use of "he" with "she" and "him" with "her" to pray over individual girls)

God, I lift _____ up to you today so that You may touch his life in a way that he will never forget. I pray that he is aware of Your work in his life to an extent that he cannot deny Your calling and Your plan.

I pray that he is mindful of Your work around him and that his awareness brings a tugging for him to actively participate in what You are doing in his life, in friends lives, and in the world around him. May he be receptive to Your invitations and leading. May his joy be deep and radiate from him as light to bring joy to those around him today.

- Colossians 1:9
- Philippians 1:9-10
- 2 Corinthians 3:17-18
- Acts 17:27-28
- Revelation 4:11
- Hebrews 12:28-29

28

RHYTHM OF REST

GROUP:

God, we pray that our children learn how to rest. In the busyness of the world around them, it is easy to get caught up in work and play to the point of burn out. It is easy to skip sleep and run on "empty" for periods of time.

In a culture where being stressed out is the norm, please teach our children a different way. Teach them the value of resting in You. Teach them to take moments and days to intentionally place themselves in rest and to stop at times within their routines and do something they delight in. Teach them to take care of their body and their soul and feed both intentionally. Teach them what it means to experience holy leisure.

INDIVIDUAL:
(replace the use of "she" with "he" and "her" with "him" to pray over individual boys)

Lord, guard _____ against losing sight of what she enjoys in her work, her day, and in the people around her. Give her an awareness of when she needs to trim her day and rearrange her priorities.

Reveal to her the joy in simplifying and in stepping back to clarify her life priorities so that she might thrive more today than yesterday. Teach her how to balance so that she might find a consistent rhythm in life of rest, play, work, and rejuvenation.

May she learn to be intentional in making time for the most important things in life instead of letting life sweep her along in its current. Thank you, Lord, for _____. She is an incredibly precious treasure. Help me to see her through Your eyes today.

- Psalms 62:1
- Deuteronomy 33:12
- Psalms 116:7
- John 5:39-40
- Philippians 1:9-10

29

OUR MISSION FIELD

GROUP:

Father, as we come before you today, we thank you for the fact that You desire relationship with us. You are active in our world and You give us the opportunity to join You in what you are doing, even to the point of working through us to accomplish Your good work.

Thank you, Lord, for making our children our most obvious mission field. Thank you for placing them as a ready, waiting audience who readily soak in our example, our attitudes, and our testimony. Give us clarity as we live life in front of them.

Give us transparent hearts so that they may know the wonder of Your grace and the transforming power of Your love. May our lives be a living testimony today of You.

May our children be protected from over-exposure to our personal hurts, bad habits, and hang-ups. May they only see how You use imperfect vessels to glorify You and accomplish Your will on this earth. May we be faithful to teach our children today, both in words and example.

May we be inspired to be better people because of the call You have placed on our lives to be living examples to them. May we be responsive to Your leading today as we interact with them.

INDIVIDUAL:
(replace the use of "he" with "she" and "him" with "her" to pray over individual girls)

Father, may I see _____ as the most important person I can witness to or disciple in the world today. May I realize that there is no mission trip to any foreign country or inner city project that is more important than the mission in my home and in _____'s life.

May I give thought to my example before him. May I give weight to his needs from me. May I see the importance today of my relationship with him and how it shapes his view of You. Shower our relationship with Your grace so that my inadequate attempts are fruitful and multiply so that we might both grow to know You more today.

- Deuteronomy 6:5-9
- Deuteronomy 31:6
- John 15
- Ephesians 2; Ephesians 4
- Philippians 4
- Colossians 3:12
- Proverbs 20:7

30

LEARNING TO BE MINDFUL AND PRESENT

GROUP:

Lord, as we watch the seasons of life pass, we are reminded of how quickly the years go and, sometimes, how slowly the hours pass. May we use our time with our children wisely. May we invest in them fully with no regrets. May we leave our "all" on the field of life, especially the life we live alongside our children.

We praise You that in Your divine wisdom You created physical seasons and life seasons. We praise You that in times of stress and turbulence we can say, "this too shall pass," and know that in the reflection of that difficult time we may eventually see Your hand in the pain.

We praise You that in times of abundant joy, contentment, and happiness, we can take a mental snapshot, and know that we can treasure those memories for the rest of our lives.

May we fill our mind with mental snapshots of precious moments with our children, moments where You are growing all of us, and moments when You are rejoicing with us.

Moments when You are carrying us through to the other side of the experience because we don't have the strength to get through it on our own. May we live in authenticity with our children, giving them a framework for understanding Your work in our world and in our lives today.

INDIVIDUAL:
(replace the use of "she" with "he" and "her" with "him" to pray over individual boys)

Father, be with _____ today as she walks through her day. May she have a growing awareness of Your presence in her life in each and every moment that she needs it today. May she learn to recognize Your hand, both in her pain and in her joy and happiness. May she be grateful for the security in life that only You can provide. May she learn that she can fully depend on You.

- Psalms 146:6
- Ecclesiastes 3:1-8
- Proverbs 2:1-10

31

PRECIOUS TREASURE

GROUP:

Father, we thank you for the children in our lives. We recognize that they are not there by chance, but for a purpose. May we be intentional today in how we interact with our children. May we communicate to them that they are the most precious treasures we will ever have here on earth.

May we treat them with the worth and value that You place on them, and may we be faithful to do our part in shaping their behavior and turning them toward You. We have prayed for these children diligently, Lord.

We place them at Your feet with full understanding that You truly desire to see them grow, thrive, and be fruitful even more than we do. They are Yours. They have been given to us to shepherd, but let us never mistake whose they really are, Lord. They are Yours.

May we be faithful to care for them, love them, nurture them, guide them, discipline them, and treasure them. May we recognize the responsibility You have placed before us, the mission we have accepted, and may we respond fully to Your call today.

INDIVIDUAL:
(replace the use of "he" with "she" and "him" with "her" to pray over individual girls)

Father God, I remember the day that You placed _____ in my life. I see now that it wasn't by chance that he appeared in my life. It wasn't by accident. It was by Your hand that he came into my life.

Thank you for blessing me with a relationship with _____. I recognize him today as Your precious treasure. I recognize him as a gift from You in my life. Give me the wisdom to lead him and guide him today so that he might know more of You.

Pour Your Spirit into my life today Lord so that my heart might be full and transparent and useful in _____'s life today. May I respond in grace and love today to those around me, and especially to _____. May I see with Your eyes what he needs from me today. May I lead him in such a way that he seeks to anchor himself to You, that he embraces life's adventures, and builds his life on the solid foundation of Your love so that he might successfully weather the storms and joys that come his way today. Thank you for placing _____ in my life. I am blessed to know him.

- I Chronicles 16:8-12
- Psalms 136:23-26

ABOUT AMY VAUGHAN

Amy's most precious treasure is her family. She is the wife of John, her partner in this fun life adventure. She is the mother of four children, who are her delight and inspiration. Amy is passionate about living life to the fullest, children, helping others, sand volleyball, and reading.

Amy is a nationally registered and Missouri State licensed occupational therapist. She is Board Certified in Pediatrics through the National Board of Certification in Occupational Therapy (NBCOT) and has practiced as a pediatric therapist for 18 years. She is a speaker, writer, and clinician in Springfield, Missouri.

She has authored other books, including "Positively Sensory! A Guide to Help Your Child Develop Positive Approaches to Learning and Cope with Sensory Processing Difficulty."

Made in the USA
San Bernardino, CA
19 February 2015